BEYOND THE WHISTLE

~31 PLAYS THAT WIN~

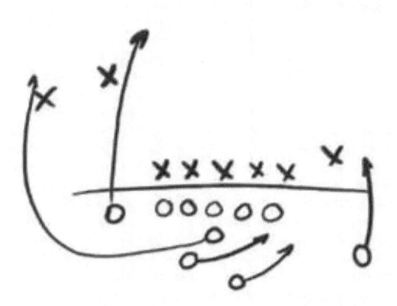

By
Ty Ford

Full Circle Publishing
PO BOX 8549
Biloxi, MS 39535
www.juliekeene.com

Printed in the United States of America

First Printing, 2017

ISBN-13: 978-0692954089
ISBN-10: 0692954082

ORDERING INFORMATION:

Quantity Sales: Special discounts are available on quantity purchases by corporations, associations, and others via
www.tyford.org

Book Cover Design: Full Circle Publishing
Book Layout & Design: Daniel Stombaugh
Proofing & Editing: Full Circle Publishing

INTRODUCTION

My name is John Tyson Ford and I am better known as "Ty." I have searched and searched over the years to find the need for my "inner man". It has been a long search but I have recently found more than what all I was looking for. His name is Jesus and through His Word, meditation upon it, and prayer; I have had "revelation" after "revelation" after "revelation".

This book of daily devotions is for you to share in several of the "revelations" I myself have had. The revelations I encounter are worth more than I can explain. It takes "time" to build a relationship. The more time put into a relationship the better it will turn out and the more benefits there are to reap.

One day, I was cutting grass nearly 4 hours and for about an hour of that I prayed in the Spirit to our Lord. When I quit, I said, "Ok Lord I have said all I can say so now I want to hear what You have to say." He responded by telling me this: "Son, you love me so much because of what you have 'read,' 'heard,' and 'experienced'. So, continue reading, keep listening, and the more you will also experience. In doing this, you will not only love Me much more, but you will also realize how much more I love you. This will only be a glimpse of how much I really love you!" What a strong revelation to hear from God! I praised Him and praised Him for this revelation!

I heard this a month ago and I am still going strong because of this that I heard. Tune into the frequency of open communication between you and God so that you may have the relationship He made you for. Enjoy these next 31 days and you may even use this 31 day devotional guide for each month over and over! Digest it every single day! May our Lord, Jesus Christ be with you always and forever.

Sincerely,
Ty

Day 1

"Cast your burden on the Lord [releasing the weight of it] and He will sustain you; He will never allow the [consistently] righteous to be moved (made to slip, fall, or fail)."

~Psalm 55:22 (AMP)

The earth does not carry any man or woman that has not been carrying burdens themselves. We all have burdens, whether small or big. We all have problems. However, there is a solution to every problem. We may tend to focus on the problems so much that they become perceived as bigger to us than the actual solution. But, the solution is always much bigger!

There are many times we carry burdens that we shouldn't even be carrying in the 1st place! It is hard to allow ourselves to give our burdens up at times. It's ordinary to carry your burdens all to yourself, wear a smile, and act as if nothing is wrong. But, that's not what The Lord wants us to do. He wants us to be faithful to Him so that when we are carrying burdens we can give them to Him and be sustained instead of shaken. Good people want to help others in this world. Good people go to other 3rd World Countries and serve the people over there to help them. Good people lend their friends money or maybe even help pay their bills because they can and are willing to help. I must tell you that we have a GOOD GOD. He is our Jehovah!

He provides. He heals. He even puts it on people's hearts to be "good" so other people's burdens may be lifted. Some people pay a stranger's light bill just to help them out, but also because God led them to do it!

1

God moves in people that are not even saved to do extraordinary things at times! God is good, and He is good all the time! The thief comes to steal, kill, and destroy but Jesus tells us that He has come to give us life in all its fullest! (John 10:10 reference) What burden are you carrying right now!? It's heavy, isn't it? Well, the burden of Christ is light and His yoke is easy (Matthew 11:30 reference). It is wiser to carry the light burden Christ offers instead of carrying the weight of the world on our shoulders all the time, which is much heavier.

Accept God's will. Surrender to His plan for your life. Don't worry about circumstances that seem to defeat you. Cast your burden on The Lord and He will sustain you! He will not allow you (a righteous man/woman because of your faith in Him) be moved or slip and fall! If you don't have faith at the right measure you believe that's needed, pray for more so you may be propelled through the obstacles you face in everyday life.

Now, be propelled through this day by God's empowering grace and His divine favor in your life. He is GOOD and He loves you! Aim for consistency in your commitment to Him as your Lord. Then, He will not allow you to slip and fall.

Walk in the Light and resemble Him in all you do.

Play of the Day – Faithfully pursue The Lord, and as you do, cast your burdens on Him so that you may be sustained.

Day 2

"Your Word is a lamp for my feet and a light for my path."

~Psalm 119:105 (NLT)

Have you ever been in the woods late at night with a flashlight searching for something, when all of a sudden your batteries die? You have been searching for hours and you just put new batteries in the flashlight, but for some reason they could not endure for all the time you needed them. It wouldn't be so bad if you had a few extra batteries on hand; but you don't! I have searched for meaning in life with all the right resources for 25 years. I found out how to make friends. I found out how to drive. I found out how to play sports. I found out how to work. I found out how to make money in ways that most people prefer not to try. I found out how to find satisfaction and pleasure. But satisfaction and pleasure are temporary. All that I mention here is temporary. I learned how to skate by and live a mediocre life that was centered around "satisfaction". But then I met Jesus and He fulfilled me. Satisfaction runs out, but fulfillment is forever. Luckily, it only took me 25 years to find "fulfillment".

It's taken every day for nearly 4 years from then to understand how to "steward" it. Life is a battle and there are obstacles at every corner and checkpoint. How are you possibly going to hurdle these obstacles and endure these trials? The answer is, of course, "JESUS!" How do you apply that extraordinary and powerful name to your everyday life!?

The Word of God shows us where we are by serving as a lamp unto our feet. His Word also shines light on the right path, illuminating the way we are to go. The Word shows us where we are at any given moment and in the middle of any situation, and He gives us vision for where to proceed. You must follow through with the vision in your life that is beneficial to not only just you, but for others as well. A banana tree does not eat its own fruit. It may enjoy when others eat off of it, though. For example, I enjoy bearing fruit that is beneficial to my brothers and sisters. However, I am not made to survive off my own fruit. God uses other people to help me in such a way where I bear fruit. God especially uses His Word to help me grow. His Word helps me grow just like it will help YOU grow! Allow His Word to mature you spiritually so you may become more effective physically.

In order to gain physical strength, one must have physical food. In order to gain spiritual strength, one must take in spiritual food. Become spiritually strong so that you may be influential in today's world.

There are men and women out there starving today in need of God bearing fruit. They will go hungry until you make gains from God's Word to give you substance so that you can feed them with what you learn. Our actions must line up with God's Word because 1 Peter tells us to be "set apart as holy for He is holy."

Read the Word and become saturated with it so that whenever you are questioned or squeezed, it is all that comes out of you. When you face trials, don't allow obscene language to come out. Instead, allow the goodness of God and His Word come out since that is what's mostly in you.

Play of the Day – **Study your life playbook, the Word of God, and let it guide you into the promises as you run the routes it assigns to you.**

Day 3

"And this same God who takes care of me will supply all your needs, based on His glorious riches, which have been given to us through Christ Jesus."

~Philippians 4:19 (NLT)

If a rich man says he is going to pay you based on what he has, and you know he is filthy rich, you ought to expect a fantastic pay day! God pays us based on His glorious riches, so shouldn't we understand that what we have available to us is plentiful!? Of course we should, but do we!? How on earth do we receive? How on earth do we reap portions of the glorious riches God has stored up in the Heavens? We must SOW! What does it mean to sow?

Galatians 6:7 tells us we will harvest what we plant. For example, have you ever planted seeds for plants to grow? Whether you grow day lilies, corn, or even marijuana you must put the seeds into the ground to reap a harvest of any sort. You must sow the seeds of what you wish to reap. If you wish to reap a harvest of corn, you must plant (sow) corn! If you wish to reap a harvest of day lilies, you must plant (sow) day lilies. If you wish to reap a harvest of marijuana, you must plant (sow) marijuana. I never have planted corn or day lilies but I sure have planted some marijuana in my past time! (I was addicted to marijuana for 11 years but God has delivered me from the addiction and I have been totally drug free and nicotine free since September 24, 2012). Praise God! I don't condone illegal marijuana use. I simply wish to establish common ground with all my fellow men and women. I had to do more than simply plant the seed! I had to water it and trust that the local stores had good fertilizer I could use so that it would produce an even better harvest!

First I had to put the seed in the ground for there to be any hope that it would grow. Paul, in this letter to the Philippians, thanked them for all the help they offered him and provided for him as he carried out the ministry the Lord entrusted him with. You see, those Philippians were told by Paul that they were due to receive something from the Lord in RETURN for their SOWING! We will not REAP if we do not SOW. As long as we SOW, we shall REAP.

"And let us not get tired of doing what is right for after a while we will REAP a harvest of blessings IF we do not get discouraged and give up."

~Galatians 6:9

When we sow, we must understand that sometimes we will reap instantly and other times it may take years. Therefore, we must keep sowing. We plant as many crops that we can in as many fields that are available.

Better yet, we are to sow every time there is an opportunity and we are capable because that opportunity is as prime as a field of fertile soil. If you sow money into a ministry and do it cheerfully, you have a harvest that awaits you. God will outdo you every time! It may be neither the way you anticipate nor the time frame you are expecting, but He is faithful to do as He promises no matter how much it may cost! We can sow so much that it gets out of control, but guess what!? God will give back to you beyond what you sowed by far! I listened to a sermon on sowing and reaping on my way back from a trip. I was led to buy cokes for the kitchen crew at Mercy House. I spent nearly $13 and immediately reaped a $10 gift card to a gas station as I checked out to buy the cokes! The next day a friend bought me a $9 lunch! God is good! And, He is good all the time.

I speak a plentiful harvest into existence for all of your lives immediately after you begin this wonderful adventure of sowing into other people's needs as well as churches and ministries that are in need. May the very same God who provides for me bless you, too. In Jesus Christ wonderful Name may you receive!

Play of the Day – Don't be afraid to sow into the lives of others your time, talent, and treasure. As you do, you're investing into the Kingdom of God, and He will surely reward you.

PLAYS THAT WIN

SOW EVERY TIME THERE IS AN OPPORTUNITY AND WE ARE CAPABLE BECAUSE THAT OPPORTUNITY IS AS PRIME AS A FIELD OF FERTILE SOIL.

Day 4

"For those who exalt themselves will be humbled and those who humble themselves will be exalted."

~Luke 14:11 & 18:14

You are getting ready to take off on a road trip with some business friends of yours. The Assistant Director of your company is driving and you are a new employee just along for the ride. Your boss, better known as the Executive Director, is going on the trip as well. There are 2 more employees riding that have been in the company for some odd years. Would you hop in the front seat and ride shotgun? If you did, how do you think the Executive Director (your boss) would respond? You would probably be told to move to the back seat! Wouldn't it be better to choose to sit in the back and your boss insist that you sit in the front seat? It is better to humble yourself and be exalted, rather than to exalt yourself and be humbled to the extreme of humiliation.

To be humbled by force is almost humiliating. It truly can be! If I humble myself, then I am following Christ while also avoiding the embarrassment of humiliation. God will humble us by circumstances that we find unpleasant. However, He won't have to if we hold our own selves accountable by remaining humble. It is much better to be exalted by God than it is to be humbled by Him. It is much more enjoyable to choose humility ourselves rather than face God's wrath. Pride is the opposite of humility, and it leads to destruction. But, humility precedes honor.

I washed a man's feet that was paralyzed one night and the very next day received a promotion within God's Kingdom at Mercy House Ministries. I received the grace it took in order to wash this poor man's feet. God gave me all I needed in order to carry out such a humbling task.

God gave me comfort in doing this. I humbled myself to do it and God gave me the strength in order to do it. What would have happened if I told the man no? I would have felt bad and God would have humbled me forcefully by some unpleasant consequences. The conviction would have eaten me up and the discipline would have caused me to learn the hard way. It is better to be humble and become exalted than to exalt yourself and become humbled.

Have a blessed day! And, remember to be a servant today. As you make that choice the overflow of God's blessings will shower you continuously!

Play of the Day – **Live a life of continuous humility so that you may be empowered to live a life of constant promotion.**

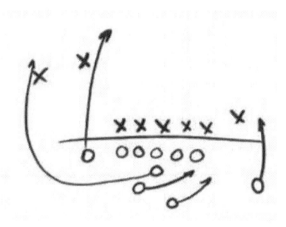

Day 5

"And do not bring sorrow to God's Holy Spirit by the way you live. Remember, he has identified you as his own, guaranteeing that you will be saved on the day of redemption."

~Ephesians 4:30 (NLT)

Sometimes we have to just HOLD ON! In times of distress it becomes a natural inclination of ours to "react" abruptly rather than "pause before responding." In my personal relationship with God, I find it more troubling to react abruptly to distress than it is to pause before responding wisely. My out-of-order conduct in such reactions multiplies my problems from "little-to-much."

"My dear brothers and sisters, be quick to listen, slow to speak, and slow to get angry. For your anger can never make things right in God's eyes."

~James 1:19-20

This walk with God is full of trials; and in our trials there tends to be lessons learned. The lessons we truly learn from are typically learned the hard way through trying circumstances. But in our trials our faith becomes tested. Abraham became a man of great faith after it was tested. He nearly killed his son that was a promise from God simply because that's what God told him to do. However, He also had faith in God to "provide" the sacrifice! It was with that faith, God provided a ram to sacrifice instead of Isaac, Abraham's son. Abraham was instructed by God to go to the land of Moriah and sacrifice his son on a mountain. Abraham followed through with obedience but somewhere in the midst of his trying circumstances he had faith in God for a bigger plan. He even told his servants that him and the boy were going to travel

11

a little farther, for them to stay put, him and the boy would worship there, then they would "both "come right back. When Isaac and Abraham reached the mountain, Isaac saw his father had the fire and wood but was asking his father where the sheep to sacrifice was. His father, Abraham said, "God will provide a sheep for the burnt offering my son."

There was faith being tested in Abraham and regardless of how fearful he might have been on the inside, his actions exemplified great faith and God blessed him abundantly for it!

Read Genesis 22. In this journey we are called to step out on great faith and live a radical life in obedience to our Heavenly Father. When we fail to do this, it grieves the Holy Spirit in our lives which robs us of the fulfillment that obedience has to offer. Satisfaction is like drinking water when thirsty repeatedly over the course of a lifetime. But "fulfillment" is the result of a one time commitment that's kept up with over a lifetime!

Play of the Day – **Rather than reacting to life's problems with impulsiveness, rely on God's grace to respond faithfully. Be obedient, trust in The Lord, and don't grieve the Holy Spirit.**

Day 6

"And if one member suffers, all the parts [share] the suffering; if one member is honored, all the members [share in] the enjoyment of it."

~1 Corinthians 12:26 (AMP)

Some "feel" like the Holy Spirit attracts unity but truthfully that's backwards. It is the other way around. "Unity attracts the Holy Spirit."

"You yourselves like living stones are being built up as a spiritual house, to be a holy priesthood, to offer spiritual sacrifices acceptable to God through Jesus Christ."

~1 Peter 2:5

We as the Body of Christ are all like "living stones" being built up as a spiritual house. We are to be united. When we are united we empower the Holy Spirit to show out!!! On the Day of Pentecost, 120 believers were united and on one accord gathered together in one place. It was then that there was a sound from Heaven, like the roaring of a mighty windstorm, and it filled the house where they were sitting. It was then that what looked like flames or tongues of fire appeared and settled on them. It was then that everyone present was filled with the Holy Spirit and began speaking other languages, as the Holy Spirit gave them this ability (Acts 2). What testimony would this have been if the Holy Spirit did all of this without anyone present in that upper room? There would have not been any kind of Testimony because no one would have been there to witness it. Therefore, the power of the Holy Spirit operates through "unity."

If one member of the "Christ following" body suffers and carries burdens, the rest of the body is called to share in their suffering. The

Body of Christ is meant to be one. We are all members of this body. If your arm hurts, your brain registers and processes that pain. And it is up to the other arm to take some loads off of the one that is in pain.

You see as Christ is the Head, it is up to the other members of the body to be in tune with what is being processed up there at the head. When we are in tune with the Holy Spirit, we are in constant fellowship with Christ, Who is the Head. In that, we recognize His leading and commands.

What He is processing will signal us to take action accordingly. For example, a member of Christ's Body is suffering, so Christ takes account for that and sends other members to help lighten the load from that one member.

In this there is unity. In unity there is power. With power there is strength. With strength there is force. A body on one accord is an unstoppable force!

Play of the Day – **Refuse to create denominational barriers that create division. Seek love above all else and be in unity with other believers. Don't focus on what you disagree about. Concentrate on the fact that you both love Christ and desire His will to be done on earth as it is in Heaven.**

Day 7

"But Ruth replied, "Don't ask me to leave you and turn back. Wherever you go, I will go; wherever you live, I will live. Your people will be my people, and your God will be my God. Wherever you die, I will die, and there I will be buried. May The Lord punish me severely if I allow anything but death to separate us!" When Naomi saw that Ruth was determined to go with her, she said nothing more."

~Ruth 1:16 - 1:18 (NLT)

What was it like when you had given your entire life to Christ? After salvation, what else is it that we could possibly want? When you got saved, did your priorities change? Or are they still the same? I know once I got saved I no longer bargained with God in order to manipulate my way through life dodging all the difficult routes. I began to instead pray for the equipping processes like sanctification, consecration, and circumcision of the heart to take place. I wanted the anointing that the Spirit of God carries in order that "life" and "salvation" may be brought to others. I got to the point where I made a commitment to go wherever He went despite the difficulties that such a journey consisted of. He was always so faithful to me and once I realized just how faithful He had always been, it inspired me to also be faithful to Him.

"But if you refuse to take up your cross and follow Me, you are not worthy of being Mine. If you cling to your life you will lose it. But if you give it up for Me you will find it."

~Matthew 10:38-39

When I gave up my life and took up my cross to follow Him, the possibilities and opportunities all of a sudden became "infinite" and "eternal." I gave up a lesser life to inherit an "abundance" of life.

Naomi was Ruth's mother in law. Naomi had two sons (Mahlon and Kilion) and a husband named Elimelech. Her husband had died followed by the death of both her sons 10 years later. So, she was rich and full, but then became a widow. Widows back in that day were taken advantage of and ignored. They were almost always poverty stricken. God's law was for the nearest relative of the dead husband to care for the widow; but Naomi had no relatives in Moab, and she did not know if any of her relatives were alive in Israel. However, Naomi was on a mission to go back to Israel to find out what family she still had left there. Both daughter-in-laws had left with her to begin with. But soon after their departure, Naomi displayed a selfless attitude nearly demanding they both turn around and go back in hopes for the security of another marriage for each of them. Orpah, one of her daughter-in-laws, had taken her up on her offer to turn around and go back. But, not Ruth. She had decided to stay. Ruth gave up the hope of security to face the fear of the unknown. She remained loyal to her mother-in-law, Naomi, and was tremendously blessed for it. She became a great-grandmother of King David and a direct ancestor of Jesus. She was not disqualified because of her race, sex, or national background. She was a Moabite, but that didn't stop her from worshipping the Spirit of the Living God. Ruth belonged to a nation that was often despised by Israel. However, her commitment to being faithful far surpassed her fear of rejection. Her faith was in God while not even God's chosen people approved of her. However, her faith was not compromised because of other's opinions.

Following God, becoming faithful to Him, and remaining loyal to relationships are difficult. However, whenever we are called to do something that seems impossible, God gives us the grace to do it. The impossibilities in life become realities to us as grace is provided by God!

Play of the Day – **Let your commitment to being faithful outweigh your fear of rejection.**

Day 8

"And Jesus, looking upon him, loved him, and He said to him, You lack one thing; go and sell all you have and give [the money] to the poor, and you will have treasure in heaven; and come [and] accompany Me [walking the same road that I walk]."

~Mark 10:21 (AMP)

What holds us back from following Jesus with our "all"? Is it our time? Is it our schedules? Is it our money? Is it fear? Is it the motives of our heart?

Whatever it is, we must pray for these roadblocks to be exposed. Then, we can break through these obstacles and Jesus may have our "all"! So what "one thing" is it you lack? I pray in Jesus Name that whatever it is, it be revealed to you today. In order to fulfill the call God has on your life, you must become centered in "His perfect will". That only comes by allowing God to remove the hindrances and distractions in our lives that are separating us from His perfect will.

There is the "permissive will of God", and the "perfect will of God". Permissive will is simply doing things for God that gets us by. However, this can lead to disappointments and other roadblocks because if all we are doing for God is getting us by, there is a bare minimum of fruit produced in our lives.

"A good (healthy) tree cannot bear bad (worthless) fruit, nor can a bad (diseased) tree bear excellent fruit [worthy of admiration]. Every tree that does not bear good fruit is cut down and cast into the fire."

~Matthew 7:18 - 7:19 (AMP)

17

Obviously, we want to be good stewards of time, schedules, and money God blesses us with. There is the law of "re-supply" in Galatians 6 that makes us aware that what we sow we will also reap, and what we plant we will harvest. Therefore, when we sow our money into the Kingdom of God we will also reap money from that same Kingdom we sowed into.

"He who supplies seed to the sower and bread for food will supply and multiply your seed for sowing and increase the harvest of your righteousness."

~2 Corinthians 9:10

I challenge you, as a reader of this devotion, to allow God to expose the hindrances and distractions there are in your life that keep you from being centered in God's "perfect will".

God's perfect will is good and acceptable. God's perfect will is doing exactly what it is He put you on this earth to do. You may be feeding the homeless once a month. And that is a wonderful way to serve God!

It may be the "perfect will" for some, and "permissive will" for others. But, what if He is calling you to do so much more than just that? Jesus Himself tells us all in Matthew 28:19, 20 "Go therefore and make disciples of all nations, baptizing them in the name of the Father and of the Son and of the Holy Spirit, teaching them to observe all that I have commanded you. And behold, I am with you always, to the end of the age." He is calling us to get to know Him, follow His ways, become more obedient to Him, and also teach others what He has taught us.

We are called to disciple others under His command of this Great Commission. We may be feeding the homeless and that may be exactly where we are supposed to be. But, are we sharing the love of Christ and discipling those who are in desperate need of godly direction? Are we in the right place, but falling short of what we are doing with the souls that surround us in that particular environment?

As Pastor of Fourth Day Ministries with a house used to help transition those in recovery, I have learned that housing men, getting them jobs, and helping them manage their money does not fulfill the purposes God has for me in this side of the transitional ministry. I have come to discover that there is much more to it than just that! God's purposes for this transitional ministry are much greater. He has chosen me to lead these men, "father" them, and raise them up as "sons"! He has called us to disciple them so they may be empowered to disciple others!

Even in just that, there is always room for much improvement in how we treat these men, teach them, and love them. Then God looks at our heart's motives in all that we do and all that we say. There isn't any room for "complacency". However, there is plenty of room for God to expose the hindrances in our lives. This is necessary to help us discern that one thing we lack that interferes with giving God our all! Go deeper with The Lord today and be blessed! Be a blessing to others by loving God and loving people.

Play of the Day – Seek God with your all. Allow Him to expose the areas of your life that are unfruitful and lacking so that you may allow God to strengthen you in those areas and become more fruitful.

PLAYS THAT WIN

BE A SERVANT TODAY. AS YOU MAKE THAT CHOICE, THE OVERFLOW OF GOD'S BLESSINGS WILL SHOWER YOU CONTINUOUSLY!

Day 9

"So now I am giving you a new commandment: Love each other. Just as I have loved you, you should love each other. Your love for one another will prove to the world that you are My disciples."

~John 13:34,35

We are called by Jesus Christ, Himself, to love others the way He loves us. This command pierces deep through the heart and grips the soul.

This command aggravates the flesh. But, the only way we can even come close to obeying this command is by allowing the Holy Spirit to empower us to do so. The heart is deceitful above all things and desperately wicked so who could possibly know their heart well enough to draw strength from it in order to carry out a holy and pure command?

(Jeremiah 17:9 influenced)... Loving others the way God loves you is an impossible command to carry out if the source where your love comes from is "desperately wicked".

We may be able to carry out some "external" signs of love *occasionally* with our hearts, but not consistently. We must know where our strength comes from! Our Father in Heaven has an unlimited supply of **love** for us to receive while the Holy Spirit has the power to receive this love and distribute it to others wisely and unconditionally. When we get *saved* by *receiving the free gift of salvation by faith*, we have peace with God. In that peace, we then *receive* a "heart transplant".

With the new heart we receive, that new heart **knows** it must draw its strength from the Holy Ghost! **In that new heart, it knows it's going to function at its best when it loves God, trusts God, and loves people**.

That new heart knows it cannot love people the way God has called it to, without drawing its strength from the Holy Spirit!

That new heart knows the **fruit of the Holy Spirit**, and knows it well. However, that new heart knows that *love, joy, peace, faithfulness, gentleness, kindness, goodness, self-control, and patience* does not come from itself; but God alone!

Play of the Day – Rely on God's Spirit to flourish in your life and provide everything you need in order to love others like Christ loves you.

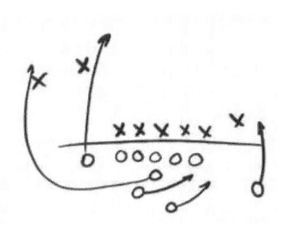

Day 10

"In view of all this, make every effort to respond to God's promises. Supplement your faith with a generous provision of moral excellence, and moral excellence with *knowing God*, and *knowing God* with self-control, and self-control with patient endurance, and patient endurance with godliness, and godliness with brotherly affection, and brotherly affection with love for everyone. The more you grow like this, the more productive and useful you will be in your knowledge of our Lord Jesus Christ."

~2 Peter 1:5 - 8 (NLT)

The Lord spoke to me concerning His love and the depth of it one evening on my way home...

He calls us to love others the way He loves us...

Furthermore, He has called me to love people the way He loves me. And He has also called you to love others the way He loves you. That is why it is so important we be intimate with The Lord and relational with others. If we are merely relational with others, yet not intimate with God, our relations with others are dry. But, with **knowing God** there is a love that is drawn from Him which is unspeakable and life changing. As He changed my life and gave me a hunger for more, I am able to **pour out** deposits He has stored into my soul! From His Spirit, I withdraw from Him and deposit this love into others.

God is no respecter of persons! Just as He makes deposits into my life so I may bless others, He will also make deposits into your life beyond what you could imagine!

23

And, as you encounter His love, you become inspired to love just like He loves! In doing so, there's no such thing as "there". But, there is always room for so much more!!!

PRAISE THE LORD!!!

He is worthy of our never-ending praise!!!

Play of the Day – Seek the Lord in such a way that you draw love from Him like a well draws water. Then, you will be more productive in all that you do.

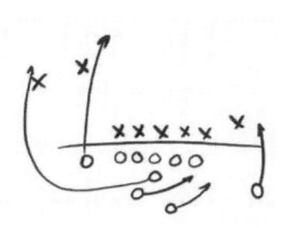

Day 11

"No power in the sky above or in the earth below – indeed, nothing in all creation will ever be able to separate us from the love of God that is revealed in Christ Jesus our Lord. "

~Romans 8:39 (NLT)

"You see son, My love for you is forever high... Is forever wide... Is forever deep... My love for you is endless! My love for you cannot be measured by a yardstick. It cannot be measured by a ruler... It cannot even be measured by miles. My love for you cannot even be measured by the word, 'infinite'.

My love for you is beyond what you can understand. My ways are higher than your ways and My thoughts are higher than your thoughts.

You see son, this is to give you a clue and insight for My love for you. My Word says to 'Love others the way I have loved you.' So since you know this love I have for you, you ought to also love others beyond what you have been.

You see son, there's no room for complacency. There is no such thing as 'there'. But, when you recognize My love for you... and you meditate on My love for you... the depth, the height, the width... the limitless love I have for you... it leads you into the assignment which is much greater than what has been previously estimated...

The assignment I have for you is to love others to a whole other level, to a whole other dimension... than you have ever been made aware.

Your love for others ought to resemble My love for you... The more love you receive from Me at the depth of a greater measure than you previously estimated before, the more accountable you are to love others much deeper, much higher, much wider, much more!

Be blessed, My son. For I love you forever, and forever, and forever... More!!!"

When the Father speaks, we must tune in, listen, and record.

"When the Spirit of truth comes, He will guide you into all truth. He will not be presenting His own ideas. He will be telling you what He has heard. He will tell you about the future."

~John 16:13

The Godhead consists of: Father, Jesus Christ, and Holy Spirit. The Holy Spirit will speak the Fathers truth to us. The Holy Spirit is our Counselor, Comforter, Strengthener, Intercessor, Helper, Advocate, and Standby. He delivers the Father's truth to us. He delivers to us the truth about Christ. He convicts us of sin, counsels us in the right direction, and strengthens us to overcome.

Play of the Day — **Receive today a fresh knowledge of God's love for you and allow it to empower you into living a life from a whole other dimension.**

Day 12

"If you love Me, obey My commandments. And I will ask the Father, and he will give you another Advocate, who will never leave you. He is the Holy Spirit, who leads into all truth. The world cannot receive Him, because it isn't looking for Him and doesn't recognize Him. But you know Him, because He lives with you now and later will be in you."

~John 14:15 - 14:17 (NLT)

Obedience to God is hard! We can't truly do it on our own. Our Father has been gracious enough to send His only begotten Son, Jesus Christ, to shed blood for 6 hours while hanging on a Cross for all people of the world including you and me! *Salvation is a free gift to be received*.

We receive this *free gift by faith* in Jesus Christ and what He has done for us on the Cross. He didn't die *for us*. He died "*as us*." He takes us as we are by means of His grace.

The purpose of the Father sending His Son, Jesus, to die on the Cross for us was to *repossess what was His all along to begin with.* How can we possibly *obey* Jesus and His teachings without the same disposition that resided in Him? We can't! That's why He left for us His helper, His advocate; the Holy Spirit.

The Holy Spirit gives us the goods necessary for empowering us to live an obedient lifestyle! The fruit of the Holy Spirit according to Galatians 5:22-23 is love, joy, peace, faithfulness, gentleness, kindness, goodness, patience, and self-control.

There is no law against these things as Scripture says. The fruit of the Holy Spirit reveals Christ-like character in our lives. The Holy Spirit gives us an unlimited supply of strength to live Christ-like lives!

Play of the Day – **Speak out loud, "I receive a fresh baptism of God's Holy Spirit and a fresh anointing." Now, let the good times roll!**

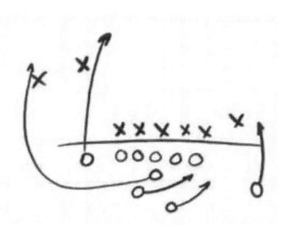

Day 13

"But you belong to God, my dear children. You have already won a victory over those people, because the Spirit who lives in you is greater than the spirit who lives in the world."

~1 John 4:4

There are many people who are "of the world" that are sent to deceive and confuse God's children. This is why it is so important to be grounded spiritually in the Word of God.

We ought to be so familiar with the Word of God that no devil in hell can deceive us! Jesus Christ came in a real body, died a real death by crucifixion on the Cross, and was really resurrected as He rose from the dead. He really did take the keys to death, hell, and the grave. He disarmed the spiritual rulers and authorities of the world publicly shaming them by His victory over them on the cross (Colossians 2:15).

Jesus Christ becomes our Savior when we recognize Him as Lord (Romans 10:9-10).

God's Word feeds us the faith we must practice in our daily lives (Romans 10:17).

The powers of hell and darkness don't stand a chance against the power of God and His light! In Exodus 12, the magicians with their worldly spiritual powers could mimic the power of God which was operating through Moses and Aaron with their staff. However, the worldly spiritual powers was no match for God! Although the staff of Aaron was up against numerous serpents of the world, the staff which was operating in the power of God swallowed up all the others which were "of the world"!

Play of the Day — Do not fear the powers of darkness but be empowered by the Holy Spirit as you remain in Christ driven by His truth!

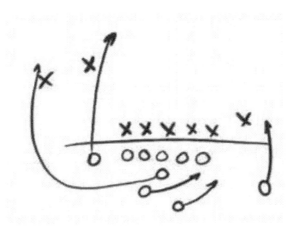

Day 14

"Work hard so you can present yourself to God and receive His approval. Be a good worker, one who does not need to be ashamed and who correctly explains the Word of Truth."

~2 Timothy 2:15

We renew our minds by reading the Word of God (Romans 12:2).

We grow in our faith through Christ by reading His Word. We discover God's will for our lives by way of His Word (Romans 12:2).

We are made right with God through our faith in Jesus Christ. Salvation is a free gift to be received by faith (Romans 4:16).

We can't work our way into obtaining salvation. It is simply a free gift from God that we receive through faith in what Christ has "done". As we grow in our knowledge and understanding of Christ, we learn that He has called us into good works and set us apart for these good works.

The Word of God must be studied consistently and diligently in order for one to be sustained in their God ordained purpose for living! God designed us all for a specific ministry. All of God's sons and daughters have been called to the ministry of reconciliation. Regardless of our day job, we are called to lead others to Christ. We do this by upholding God's standards.

We live for Christ by exemplifying Christ-like conduct. We are empowered in our living by the diligence of our learning. A life in profession to Christ will invite many questions from others who are intrigued by the light.

Therefore, we must be prayed up, studied up, and prepared to answer questions that could very well be the answer that changes a person's eternity.

Play of the Day – Study God's Word daily and cling to His truth. Understand the totality of His truth and be prepared to tell others the fullness of the Gospel!

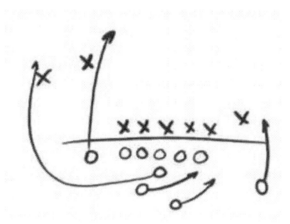

Day 15

"We know what real love is because Jesus gave up His life for us. So we also ought to give up our lives for our brothers and sisters."

~1 John 3:16

Jesus bled on a Cross for 6 hours so that people like you and me would have freedom from bondage with fulfillment taking its place. Fulfillment is far better than any satisfaction.

Fulfillment doesn't run out, but satisfaction does. Satisfaction is like chasing the wind; meaningless. Fulfillment takes place when you live out God's purpose for your life. It's significant and eternal.

Since Christ laid down His life to fulfill us, we ought to lay our lives down for others to also become fulfilled through Christ! Love covers a multitude of sins (1 Peter 4:8).

There is no greater love than for one to lay down their life for their friends (John 15:13).

Where do you live? What needs do you see? How can you meet the needs of your community or region or nation Christ's way? Pray about it. Then lay your life down with the motivation of love on your side as you meet people's needs God's way!

Play of the Day – Live a life that is in pursuit of fearlessly loving others.

PLAYS THAT WIN

WE MUST BE PRAYED UP, STUDIED UP, AND PREPARED TO ANSWER QUESTIONS THAT COULD VERY WELL BE THE ANSWER THAT CHANGES A PERSON'S ETERNITY.

Day 16

"There is no greater love than to lay down one's life for ones friends."

~John 15:13

When I lived for the world, I went above and beyond. What about you? Isn't it necessary then to go above and beyond for Christ? We must start by laying down our offenses that divide and separate us from the very love that had bound us all together through Christ and His sacrifice at the Cross initially. Offenses are walls that rise and destroy the Body of Christ!

Jesus prayed for all believers to be protected by His Name and united just as He and the Father are united (John 17:11).

We are called to overlook these offenses by forgiving one another and making allowance for each other's faults (Colossians 3:13). Love binds us all together in perfect harmony (Colossians 3:14).

We are called to serve God by serving people. Our relationship with Christ gives us the spiritual nourishment we need in order to do this from day to day. We must not drown out our private time with the Father by service. Instead, we are to spend time with the Father. And in that alone time, we receive the fresh fire from the Holy Ghost we need to continue serving Christ! We honor Christ by laying down our lives for the well-being of others!

Play of the Day – Have strong intimate time with The Lord. Make it your number 1 priority, and in that process you will be empowered to love others like you never have before.

PLAYS THAT WIN

WE MUST NOT DROWN OUT OUR PRIVATE TIME WITH THE FATHER BY SERVICE. INSTEAD, WE ARE TO SPEND TIME WITH THE FATHER... AND IN THAT ALONE TIME, WE RECEIVE THE FRESH FIRE FROM THE HOLY GHOST WE NEED TO CONTINUE SERVING CHRIST!

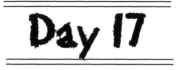

Day 17

"You will keep in perfect peace all who put their trust in You, all whose thoughts are fixed on you!"

~Isaiah 26:3

Have you ever started a project and was very confident in finishing it until your mind began to drift off into worrying?

Living the Christian life involves many seasons. Some seasons you are strong, bold, and confident. However, we all face seasons where our focus is broken and our minds begin to wander. This is where we are tested in the area of *trusting The Lord*!

Place your trust in The Lord and He will never fail you. Circumstances will not always be what you hoped for, but He won't let you down when you fix your thoughts on Him and your perception is aligned with His!

Often times we want situations to turn out a certain way, but they don't. This tests the trust we have with The Lord. However, we will never be disappointed by trusting in Him and His higher ways.

"My ways are higher than your ways and My thoughts are higher than your thoughts. For just as the heavens are higher than the earth, so are My ways higher than your ways and thoughts higher than your thoughts."

~Isaiah 55:8,9

As we fix our thoughts on Jesus and place all our trust in Him; regardless of the situation or circumstances, we will never be disappointed!

If you are disappointed at first, seek enlightenment from Him to see as He sees; and you will be comforted as your eyes are opened to another realm.

Play of the Day – **Place your trust in God, fix your thoughts on His purposes, see as He does, and you will never be let down!**

Day 18

"My dear brothers and sisters, whenever trouble comes your way let it be an opportunity for joy. For when your faith is tested, your endurance has a chance to grow. So let it grow. For when your endurance becomes fully developed, you will be strong in character and ready for anything."

~James 1:2-4

The trials we go through are often miserable to our flesh but great for our Spirit man. It's uncomfortable. It can even feel much like a short season of misery. But, when we perceive trials through God's eyes, we ought to be full of great joy because the trials are necessary to go through in order to come out stronger.

The more trials we embrace, the further from our spiritual immaturity we become. The more trials we endure, the more spiritually mature we become.

Let's face it; trials season us into who we were designed to be all along. Resembling Christ-like character requires facing many seasons of trials. For in our trials, we become new.

We are in a process of transformation. This process involves many seasons of trials. The only way to grow stronger is to face much adversity.

Adversity is a university that prepares us for the greatness, which God has called us to.

Are you excited for the trials that come your way on this special day The Lord has made?

Play of the Day – **Praise God in the storm and lean on His strength for the trials you face so that you may overcome!**

Day 19

"We can rejoice, too, when we run into problems and trials, for we know that they help us develop endurance. And endurance develops strength of character, and character strengthens our confident hope of salvation. And this hope will not lead to disappointment. For we know how dearly God loves us, because He has given us the Holy Spirit to fill our hearts with His love"

~Romans 5:3-5

The trials and problems we face in everyday life hold great value. Walking out the process of our trials is when we ought to rejoice the most. In our rejoicing, there's great joy. Great joy provides great strength (Nehemiah 8:10).

Overcoming our trials with godliness requires joy. Joy illuminates God's goodness. God is too good to allow us to go through trials He is unaware of. The teacher may be silent during the test. But, He is an "all-knowing" God. He wears many hats.

He is Jehovah Jireh, The Lord Who provides!
He is Jehovah Ropheka, The Lord Who heals!
He is Jehovah Mkkadeshkim, The Lord Who sanctifies!
He has many other hats as well.

When we're going through trials, He is aware. He may be silent during our trials. However, He still makes a way to overcome. It's when we overcome trials and problems that we develop endurance and maturity. In the process of our trials is when we are being prepared for His promises. If it weren't for our trials and problems we face daily, we would be premature for His promises.

41

The processes we face and walk out are actually equipping us to be sustained in His promises! When we discover the character of Jesus Christ, we become knowledgeable of Who He is. When we apply what we draw from His character in everyday life, we inherit His character qualities and grow in His strength.

This strength is what we need so we may boldly come to His throne as His own prized possessions without doubt or reservation!

Grow in the trials you face so you may be equipped to receive the promises of God without forfeit. Develop His strength and allow His character disposition to be produced in you. Have confidence in your salvation as you apply His Word to your everyday life and grow from it! The Lord sets trials in your path because He loves you.

Let the Holy Spirit guide you, mature you, and release His love into the lives of others from deep within you. Be blessed as you overcome through Christ Jesus. Romans 8:37 tells us that we are more than conquerors through Christ Jesus!

Play of the Day – **Release the power of the Holy Spirit from within you when you're faced with trials. He will help you endure faithfully.**

Day 20

"But if we confess our sins to Him, He is faithful and just to forgive our sins and cleanse us from all unrighteousness"

~1 John 1:9

1 John 1:8 tells us that if refuse to admit that we have sinned, the truth is not in us. When we confess our sins, yet receive Christ's forgiveness, we become cleansed by the blood Jesus shed on Calvary.

Confessing our sins is not a one-time deal in order to get saved as we declare Jesus Christ as our Lord and Master. There's many times in our Christian walk that we fall short of the call. God has called us to perfection. However, perfection is a mission and a process. We reach perfection once we arrive. We are in a process of perfection until we do.

The spirit of humility is the path we must choose. God has called us all to humility. Humility is recognizing lack of strength without God. Furthermore, a humble man knows he needs God in every aspect of his life; big or small. We need our minds to be renewed daily. We need forgiveness as we pursue the call of God for our lives and fall short periodically along the way.

We must allow the Holy Spirit to convict us and make us holy. We must allow God's truth to sanctify us and manifest in our lives, giving God much glory. You must approach God's throne with boldness and humility when dealing with sin.

Boldness because of knowing His nature and character.
Humility, because without the blood of Jesus Christ there is no forgiveness. But praise God!

"**For Christ gave His life to free us from every kind of sin, to cleanse us, and make us His very own people totally committed to doing what's right**"

~Titus 2:14

We are not yet perfect, although we relentlessly pursue it and believe in its guarantee. However, we have been transformed from carelessness into being totally committed to doing what's right! Thank God for forgiveness all along the way as we need it. God is good. He is wonderful all the time!

Play of the Day – **Continuously allow the Holy Spirit to convict you of sin so that you may repent and be restored. Engage yourself in the transformation process where you go from glory to glory and faith to faith.**

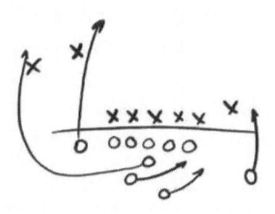

Day 21

"They threw down their staffs, which also became serpents! But then Aaron's staff swallowed up their staffs"

~Exodus 7:12

This is a prime example how the favor of God is stronger and more powerful than any army that opposes His plans! Greater is He in you than those who are in the world outside (1 John 4:4).

You may be outnumbered. But with God on your side, who really stands a chance? We live in a demon infested world where all kinds of ungodly nonsense is "socially acceptable". But, the justice of God will prevail, although it may not always seem that way. In the end every knee will bow and every tongue shall confess that Jesus is Lord (Romans 14:11 & Isaiah 46:23).

When we are living for The Lord, we will face persecution and we will have much opposition from the demonic. However, be encouraged! God is for you. He is your shelter. He is your refuge. He is your strength. If you have doubts about where you stand with God, repent. Recognize the power of His blood. Receive forgiveness. Let your conscience be cleansed. Confront life and all its obstacles with the favor and countenance of the Father on your side!

"Though a thousand fall at your side, though ten thousand are dying around you, these evils will not touch you. Just open your eyes, and see how the wicked are punished."

~Psalm 91:7-8

45

God has a wonderful plan for your life (Jeremiah 29:11).

Although there's much opposition, Jesus is our physician. We are confronted by the dark forces of the world, yet His strength empowers us for a journey of continuous victories! There's victory in Jesus. There's healing in His blood and deliverance in His Name. Jesus is the Name above all names. It is by His grace and goodness that we are sustained. Trust in Him and He will deliver you, provide the healing you need, give you victory, and make your paths straight.

Play of the Day – **Be bold and courageous! For The Lord Who watches over you is much bigger than any devil from hell!**

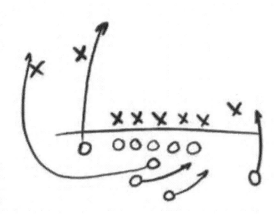

Day 22

"If you make the Lord your refuge, if you make the Most High your shelter, no evil will conquer you; no plague will come near your home."

~Psalm 91:9 - 10

Who is your god? What do you spend most of your time doing? Is The Lord Jesus Christ, Who is the Most High your God? Or, is your god an electronic device? Is your god the vehicle you drive, or the relationship you esteem so highly? Is your favorite preacher your god, or is he/she a vessel God uses to provide for you direction?

Give your leaders room for mistakes and don't put them, or anyone else, or any other thing, on a pedestal they don't belong on. Examine your priorities and evaluate yourself. Then make sure The Lord is your refuge in Whom you trust the most!

Psalm 118:8 is the center of God's Word and it says: **"Better to take refuge in The Lord than to trust in people."**

The best way to find yourself in the center of God's will is to understand what's written in the center of His Word.

When we seek the Kingdom of God and place it above all else, we will have all the protection we need. As we take a brutally honest assessment as to what we spend most of our time doing and cast down all images, thoughts, objects, and figures that exalt themselves above God; we receive shelter from the Most High. What we take refuge in, is what our shelter becomes.

If pornography is your refuge, you have no shelter.

If your pastor is your refuge, your shelter is limited.

If work is your refuge, your salary can only cover you so far.

If that relationship with your soon to be spouse is your refuge, you're endangered.

If your knowledge is your shelter, your own understanding will only get you so far.

But, when you trust in The Lord and make Him your refuge, no evil will conquer you, no plague will come near your home, and your path will be directed by Him.

Play of the Day — **Make God your shelter and place all your trust in Him, regardless of what circumstances look like. For we walk by faith and not by sight.**

Day 23

"If I could speak all the languages of earth and of angels, but didn't love others, I would only be a noisy gong or a clanging cymbal."

~1 Corinthians 13:1 (NLT)

When we learn how to love people when they are difficult is when God stretches us the most. That stretch is necessary for maturity. Therefore, when your life circumstances involve people who are difficult to love, be encouraged to step up to the plate and love them more!

For it is a step closer to maturity. Jehovah Jireh is The Lord Who provides the necessary means to do His will, on His terms, and His way! His will is to love the broken ones. His way is to love others the way He loves you (John 13:34,35).

He calls us to love others with passion, purpose, and tenacity. This proves to the world that we are disciples of His. It's impossible to love like God loves without surrender to Him. In this surrender, there's a submission that says, "I agree to be inconvenienced and love others greater."

Play of the Day – Live this day as if it's your last. Allow yourself to be inconvenienced for the sake of showing love to others. There's no greater love than to do this!

PLAYS THAT WIN

JESUS IS THE NAME ABOVE ALL NAMES. IT IS BY HIS GRACE AND GOODNESS THAT WE ARE SUSTAINED. TRUST IN HIM AND HE WILL DELIVER YOU, PROVIDE THE HEALING YOU NEED, GIVE YOU VICTORY, AND MAKE YOUR PATHS STRAIGHT.

Day 24

"I pray that from His glorious, unlimited resources He will empower you with inner strength through His Spirit"

~ Ephesians 3:16 (NLT)

When you give your life to Christ and surrender to Him, you become empowered by the Holy Spirit to live a lifestyle that resembles Christ!

We are not to be conformed to the world and its ways, but transformed by the renewing of our minds, and empowered by the Holy Spirit (Romans 12:2 & Ephesians 3:16).

Nothing is impossible with God (Luke 1:37). Therefore, we must rely on glorious and limitless resources in order to defeat the obstacles that stand in our way!

What we *see* may portray itself as an obstacle too difficult to overcome. However, we walk by *faith* not sight (2 Corinthians 5:7).

The bigger the battle, the greater the victory! The bigger the test, the more powerful the testimony! The more difficult the obstacles, the more glory for God at the time of triumph! We become strengthened by the Holy Spirit with inner strength that provides for us the tenacity to overcome external obstacles that threaten our inner peace. When your car breaks down, it can cause you to become either fearful or angry. However, the inner strength that the Holy Spirit gives us empowers us with a peace on the inside that cannot be corrupted by circumstances on the outside! Our circumstances of everyday life may test our patience and test our peace. But, God lives in us and He's not hindered by our trials. In fact, it's only because of His strength that we are able to conquer life's daily battles faithfully. Since He is able, we are able.

He works through our *availability* in making a way when there seems to be no way! When the Israelites escaped Egypt, The Lord parted the sea and made a dry path for them to be set free from their bondage in Egypt (Exodus 14:21-22).

God will do whatever it takes to set you free as long as you make yourself available to Him. When you are caught up in the darkness, make yourself available to His light and receive life more abundantly.

When obstacles threaten you, make yourself available to His glorious and unlimited resources so that you will be empowered with the inner strength you need to overcome those obstacles through the power of His Holy Spirit. There's power in the Name of Jesus! There's victory by way of His Holy Spirit!

Play of the Day – **Hold your belly and say, "Out of my belly shall flow rivers of living water!" Be empowered by His Spirit as you journey through this day!**

Day 25

"We are all infected and impure with sin. When we display our righteous deeds, they are nothing but filthy rags."

~Isaiah 64:6

We must recognize our importance, or lack thereof, without the blood covering of Jesus Christ. Our righteousness without Christ is like that of "filthy rags", by which the original Hebrew text means "menstrual garment"! That's what we all are like without the grace of God. However, we are the righteousness of God through Christ Jesus! Since Christ gave His life for those who were lost, we might become the righteousness of God through Him (2 Corinthians 5:21). We must refrain from irrational pride as it leads to destruction (Proverbs 18:12 & James 4:6).

Humility is what qualifies us for the promotion (Luke 14:11 & Luke 18:14). Humility is recognizing our need for God protection, provision, and peace. Humility understands that without God's grace and without His favor, we are nothing. Wisdom is fearing The Lord in a manner of reverence, and understanding your identity when it is in Christ. We can then see life from His perspective rather than our own. In order to reach the lost in a broken world, we must recognize our brokenness without Him, while understanding Who gets the glory for every good thing that's ever done. We must see the world through the lens of Christ so that we might live up to the call He has on us all as minsters of reconciliation (2 Corinthians 5:18).

Play of the Day – Without Christ, we are filthy. But with Him, we are righteous. Speak out loud, "I am the righteousness of God in Christ Jesus!"

PLAYS THAT WIN

WHEN OBSTACLES THREATEN YOU, MAKE YOURSELF AVAILABLE TO HIS GLORIOUS AND UNLIMITED RESOURCES SO THAT YOU WILL BE EMPOWERED WITH THE INNER STRENGTH YOU NEED TO OVERCOME THOSE OBSTACLES THROUGH THE POWER OF HIS HOLY SPIRIT.

Day 26

"But whatever I am now, it is all because God poured out His special favor on me- and not without results. For I have worked harder than any of the other apostles; yet it was not I but God who was working through me by His grace."

~1 Corinthians 15:10

We are called on by Jesus and commanded by Him to take up our cross and follow Jesus (Matthew 10:38,39/ Luke 14:27/ Mark 8:34).

This is a tough lifestyle to relentlessly pursue and carry out. However, by the grace of God we are empowered to do so!

God was working through Paul by way of His grace. Paul went on three missionary journeys, wrote 13 letters in the Bible, was the apostle assigned to the Gentiles, and was a world traveler for Christ. He was empowered by the grace of God! The grace of God accepted him as Christian killer and transformed him into a Jesus freak world changer!

God's special favor on Paul did not go without results, but instead produced fruitful obedience. Paul worked hard. However, his labor would have been in vain without the grace of God. Since God's grace was working through him, he is a hero of faith still remembered to this day. Have you received the grace of God to inspire you, challenge you, and empower you yet?

Play of the Day - Say, "I receive the grace of God to infuse into me the power that inspires fruitful obedience just as it had done with Paul! I trust in the grace of God to change me and sustain me into righteous living that gives God all the glory! Thank You Holy Spirit for infusing Your grace into me!"

PLAYS THAT WIN

THERE ISN'T ANY ROOM FOR "COMPLACENCY." HOWEVER, THERE IS PLENTY OF ROOM FOR GOD TO EXPOSE THE HINDRANCES THERE ARE IN OUR LIVES. THIS IS NECESSARY TO HELP US DISCERN THAT ONE THING WE LACK THAT INTERFERES WITH GIVING GOD OUR ALL!

Day 27

"And when he took the scroll, the four living beings and the twenty-four elders fell down before the Lamb. Each one had a harp, and they held gold bowls filled with incense, which are the prayers of God's people."

~Revelation 5:8 (NLT)

Your prayers to God are not taken lightly by Him. They are taken seriously by all who reside in the Kingdom of Heaven. "Gold" is perceived as a commodity of great value.

A "harp" played in a heavenly kind of way illustrates an atmosphere of great peace. All 24 elders fall down before the Lamb and every single one of them have a harp to play. The prayers of God's people are the "incense" that's brought to God in a gold bowl as 24 elders play a harp at The Lord's feet, near His throne of glory! Your prayers to God and all of Heaven are a big deal, needless to say.

Therefore, exercise your right to pray as His child. A child of God has an heirship to all that God owns. That's part of being a joint heir of Christ bought by His blood. The best part of being His child is the relationship it entails. God is extremely involved in our lives. Think about someone you really care about writing you a letter. This letter lets you know how they are doing. You don't take it lightly because you love them. However, the atmosphere isn't exactly the same.

You may love that friend of yours and open every letter with extreme joy and zeal! But, there's no love like the love of The Lord.

When The Lord hears your cries, receives your prayers, and tends to your needs; it's a special occasion in all of Heaven. And, for that one moment all of Heaven is focused on caring for you!

Play of the Day – Exercise your right to pray. It's a special offering brought to His throne!

Day 28

"Don't worry about anything; instead, pray about everything. Tell God what you need, and thank Him for all he has done. Then you will experience God's peace, which exceeds anything we can understand. His peace will guard your hearts and minds as you live in Christ Jesus."

~Philippians 4:6 - 4:7(NLT)

God will take our burdens. His Word tells us to cast our cares to Him (Psalm 55:22).

The Lord is faithful. He takes our weaknesses; and through them He exemplifies His strengths (2 Corinthians 12:9).

He takes our worries as He hears our prayers and sustains us. When we are overburdened, He tells us to come to Him and we will find rest because His yoke is easy and His burden is light (Matthew 11:28-29).

He tells us to not worry about tomorrow for tomorrow will bring its own worries but today's trouble is enough for today (Matthew 6:34).

He tells us that as long as we focus on His Kingdom and make that our primary concern, He will provide our every need (Luke 12:31).

Since our relationship with Christ is above all else, that relationship demands communication. The best communication involves transparency and intimacy. When we get real with God and stop trying to hide the very things He already sees and already knows, He becomes very real to us! God's not looking for a one night stand. He's demanding a relationship that's intimate, transparent, eternal, and real.

He wants us to not worry about anything, and to pray about everything. He wants us to not take Him for granted for all He's already done, but to give thanks instead, and experience His peace. His peace is far above and beyond any other peace as it far surpasses what the human mind can possibly fathom and understand.

His peace will guard our soul gates... our eyes, our minds, our ears. His peace comes to us from His throne as a reward to our gratitude, intimacy, transparency, and prayers.

Play of the Day – Seek The Lord at His throne through the shed blood of Jesus Christ and receive His peace as you get real with Him and open up your heart to Him.

Day 29

"Keep on asking, and you will receive what you ask for. Keep on seeking, and you will find. Keep on knocking, and the door will be opened to you. For everyone who asks, receives. Everyone who seeks finds. And to everyone who knocks, the door will be opened."

~Matthew 7:7 - 7:8 (NLT)

What are you asking God for? What is it that you are seeking? What doors are you knocking on?

Whatever you ask for that is within the will of God you will receive! If you are seeking a plan outside of His will, you will find out. He is gracious enough to teach us. He is faithful to discipline us. Not every plan we search out is His will, but thank God for His gentle nudges that redirect us onto the right path. His Word is a lamp for our feet and a light for our path (Psalm 119:105),

His Word reveals to us the condition of where we are and illuminates the path we are called to. Astronauts, when on a mission to the moon, must make course corrections every 10 minutes. As we follow Christ we must also make necessary adjustments to ensure we maintain our pursuit for living in His will and following His path. When we seek His will, He is faithful to reveal it to us. Whenever you search out God's purpose for your life, you will discover.

When you pursue His will for your life, you will find. When you knock on the right doors, they will open. If you knock on the wrong doors, but are searching for the right doors, He will redirect you. When we ask God questions without anticipating His answers, and are open to all the possibilities that come with the unknown; we may clearly hear His

61

answer. Some answers we like. Others we don't. However, He remains on the Throne like it or not. And, what He says goes.

We ought to be open to His course corrections. We ought to be asking, searching, and knocking with the agenda all the same. That is His will. Anything outside of His will forfeits provision, protection, and peace. On the contrary; provision, protection, and peace are all inclusive to His will.

Are you open to His purposes for your life? Are you willing to search out His will? His purpose for your life when lived out will provide fulfillment, protect you from fear, and give you peace beyond what you can fathom. Embark on the journey now!

Play of the Day – Make the necessary adjustments as you ask, seek, and find. For The Lord will direct you. Therefore, trust Him and follow His lead no matter how it looks.

Day 30

"Don't copy the behavior and customs of this world, but let God transform you into a new person by changing the way you think. Then you will learn to know God's will for you, which is good and pleasing and perfect."

~Romans 12:2 (NLT)

The behavior and customs of this world, when copied, will duplicate the realities of hell. That's not what you want for your life. You want to discover God's will for your life. You want to live out His purpose for your life! You would rather be fulfilled than empty.

You would rather be experiencing the realities of Heaven than entangled into the darkness of hell. How do we renew our minds?

We must read God's Word. When we read God's Word, we renew our minds. And, when we renew our minds diligently without ceasing, we find transformation. Who God can and will transform you into will not discourage you, but it will empower and encourage you. You will then discover what the miraculous power of the Living God can do for you!

He can and will transform you. His Word will renew your mind and empower you to discern with His wisdom, His wonderful plan that He designed just for you! "Blessed are those who hunger and thirst for righteousness for they will be filled." (Matthew 5:6)

Be blessed with a fresh anointing, a fresh hunger for His Word, and find yourself thinking differently with a new purpose that involves so much more than you could ever find on your own.

Say, "In Jesus Name, I receive a fresh anointing that breaks all yokes of bondage. I decree a fresh hunger for righteousness. Show me Your glory God, and lead me into Your will! Amen."

Play of the Day — Renew your mind with God's Word and receive revelation of His will for your life. When you receive revelation, make the necessary steps in that direction so you can be useful for The Lord.

Day 31

"God works through different men in different ways but it is the same God who achieves His purposes through them all"

~1 Corinthians 12:6

God is the giver of all gifts. He gives each of us different spiritual gifts, which are all designed to edify the Body of Christ. Gifts are meaningless and a hindrance if not exercised with the motive of love. He gives some the gift of giving, and others wise advice. He gives others the gift of special knowledge. If you have ever had your "mail read", you'll understand how that gift operates.

He gives some the gift of healing. He gives others the gift of performing miracles. He gives some the gift of tongues and others He gives the gift of interpreting the tongues. He also gives some the gift of prophecy. Another gift He gives freely is the ability to discern whether or not what is being said comes from the Spirit of God or another spirit.

Regardless of how many gifts there are, there is only one Giver. And that's the Spirit of the Living God! The Holy Spirit flows through believers with an anointing that comes on strong while exercising in these gifts and it's empowering to the church.

These gifts are all complimentary to one another propelling a powerful combining force that inspires growth and inducts change. Let there be no competition, but instead harmony and unity so that His purposes are accomplished. Ask God which gifts He wants you to have and trust in His provision.

Play of the Day – Live the fruitful life of exercising His gifts with His love as your center point of motivation. Let His love be your greatest companion as you operate in His gift for you that inspires, encourages, and edifies others.

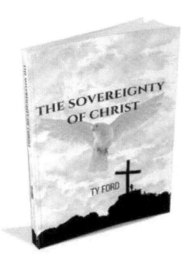

THE SOVEREIGNTY OF CHRIST

THE SOVEREIGNTY OF CHRIST is Ty's very first book and a launch into the presentation of a God given message of the power of the indwelling Holy Spirit. As believers, we accept God is all knowing but struggle in the understanding of just what that entails in our day to day life. THE SOVERIEGNTY OF CHRIST is not just a saying we throw out at the difficult times in life, this is a mindset that when understood and adopted will transform us from simply being a believer, to walking our spiritual journey as the overcomers we were designed to be. The Sovereignty of Christ is the truth that God has the authority to do what he pleases. Learn why unbelievers stumble over it and what we as believers can do to to make this understanding part of our day to day culture.

This book may be purchased at www.tyford.org
www.amazon.com

ABOUT THE AUTHOR

My name is Ty and I am a husband, father, speaker, former athlete, writer, and author of both THE SOVEREIGNTY OF CHRIST & the 31 Day Devotional, BEYOND THE WHISTLE. I have also been privileged to be the Founder and Pastor of Fourth Day Ministries. I have a passion for helping the lost find the light of God. My wife Hillary and I minister together all through the doors God opens to minister through. Currently we minister together through Fourth Day Ministries to conduct speaking events, transitional housing, and the Fellowship of Christian Athletes (FCA) where we seek to present discipleship to believers at every stage of their Christian journey. I believe God made us to be authentic in who we are and that anyone who is yielded to the Holy Spirit will see fruit in the areas God created them to bear fruit in. It is my prayer to continue, by God's grace, to be fruitful from Him and to bear fruit that remains.

-Ty

Made in the USA
Middletown, DE
08 September 2021